Authors Karen Brown & Holly Engel
Editor Linda Milliken
Assistant Editor Deneen Celecia
Designer Wendy Loreen
Illustrator Barb Lorseyedi

About the Authors

Karen Brown has been a teacher for seventeen years. She has taught learning disabled and elementary students in Lee's Summit Missouri. Karen has been a finalist in the Lee's Summit Teacher of the Year program. She is a member of the National Education Association, International Reading Association and Society of Children's Book Writers and Illustrators.

Holly Engel earned her Bachelor of Science degree from Rockhurst College in Kansas City, Missouri. She has taught elementary students in Lee's Summit, Missouri for four years. Holly has written articles for local publications, sharing her innovative classroom programs with the community and her peers. She is also a member of the National Education Association.

© 1994 **Edupress** • P.O. Box 883 • Dana Point, CA 92629

ISBN 1-56472-028-4

Table of Contents

4 *Read:*

**SAMUEL EATON'S DAY;
A DAY IN THE LIFE OF
A PILGRIM BOY**
*Follow Samuel through his busy day in the
colonial village of Plymouth.*

Responses: Pre-reading Plot Prediction   **5**
Photo Essay   **6**
Venn Diagram   **7**
Vocabulary Map   **8**
Critical Analysis   **10**
Translation Activity   **12**

---

14 *Read:*

OH, WHAT A THANKSGIVING!
*David uses his imagination to travel back in
time to experience one of the first Thanksgiving
meals. He wants his Thanksgiving to be like
one during colonial times.*

Responses: Research Activity   **15**
Comparison Chart   **16**
Paper Dolls   **18**
Invitation   **20**
Time Line   **21**
Colonial American Speech   **22**

---

24 *Read:*

**... IF YOU LIVED IN
COLONIAL TIMES**
*Find out what it was like to be a boy or girl in
the New England colonies during the years
1630 to 1730.*

Responses: KWL Chart   **25**
Law Poster   **26**
School Simulation   **28**
Jeopardy Game   **30**
Stitchery Project   **31**
Job Investigation   **32**

---

34 *Read:*

THE MATCHLOCK GUN
*In a daring plan to protect her family against
the Indians, Gertrude lures them to her home,
hoping that the instructions she gave Edward
will be listened to and save them all.*

Responses: Mock Trial   **35**
Cooking Activity   **36**
Context Clue Activity   **38**
Plot Change Diagram   **39**
Letter Composition   **41**
Character Predictions   **42**

---

44 *Read:*

A LION TO GUARD US
*When Amanda's mother dies, she decides to
take her siblings to the New World to find their
father. Bravely, they depart with only the
protection of a brass lion's head.*

Responses: Content Predictions   **45**
Character Questionnaire   **46**
Comparative Graph   **48**
Alternate Ending   **49**
Story Map   **50**
Family Shield   **52**

---

54 *Read:*

**WHO'S THAT STEPPING
ON PLYMOUTH ROCK**
*Here is the account of the adventurous life of
Plymouth Rock from the year it was stepped on
to how it was recognized to where it is today.*

Responses: Pre-reading Associations   **55**
Cause and Effect Study   **56**
Sequencing Activity   **58**
Plymouth Rock Autobiography   **60**
Team Debate   **62**
Question and Answer Activity   **63**

• *A New Look at the Pilgrims:*
Why They Came to America
by Beatrice Siegel;
Walker 1987.

• *A Williamsburg Household*
by Joan Anderson;
Ticknor 1988.

• *Calico Bush*
by Rachel Field;
Macmillan 1987.

• *Charlie's House*
by Clyde Robert Bulla;
Harper LB 1983.

• *Courage of Sarah Noble*
by Alice Dalgliesh;
Macmillan 1954.

• *The Double Life of Pocahontas*
by Jean Fritz;
Putnam 1983.

• *Fog Magic*
by Julia Sauer;
Penguin 1986.

• *Going to School in 1776*
by John J. Loeper;
Macmillan 1973.

• *If You Sailed on the Mayflower*
by Ann McGovern;
Scholastic 1970.

• *The Landing of the Pilgrims*
by James Daugherty;
Random LB 1950.

• *Molly's Pilgrim*
by Barbara Cohen;
Lothrop 1983.

• *Night Journeys*
by Avi;
Pantheon 1979.

• *Pilgrim Children Come to Plymouth*
by Ida DeLage;
Garrard LB 1981.

• *The Pilgrims of Plimoth*
by Marcia Sewall;
Atheneum 1986.

• *Sara Morton's Day:*
A Day in the Life of a Pilgrim Girl
by Kate Waters;
Scholastic 1989.

• *The Schoolmasters*
by Leonard Everett Fisher;
Godine 1986.

• *The Sign of the Beaver*
by Elizabeth George Speare;
Houghton Mifflin 1983.

• *The Thanksgiving Story*
by Alice Dalgliesh;
Macmillan 1988.

• *They Sought a New World*
by William Kurelek and Margaret S. Engelhart;
Tundra 1985.

• *This New Land*
by G. Clifton Wisler;
Walker LB 1987.

Samuel Eaton's Day

A Day in the Life of a Pilgrim Boy

by KATE WATERS

Photographs by RUSS KENDALL

SAMUEL EATON'S DAY: A DAY IN THE LIFE OF A PILGRIM BOY
by Kate Waters
Published by Scholastic, Inc., 1989.
Canadian distribution by Scholastic, Canada.

DESCRIPTION:
40 pages
Photographic journal

READING LEVEL:
Read aloud—Grades 3-4
Independent—Grades 5-6

CONTENT NOTES:

Review the content notes presented at the back of the literature selection. Samuel Eaton was an actual boy who sailed with his family on the Mayflower. The photographs were taken at Plimoth Plantation, an outdoor living history museum that portrays life as it was in seventeenth-century Plymouth, Massachusetts. Note, also, the use of colonial dialect in the text.

Sara Morton's Day: A Day in the Life of A Pilgrim Girl (Scholastic Inc.) is a photographic journal about a young girl in the same village.

CONTENT SUMMARY:

Samuel Eaton is a seven-year-old boy who lives in the growing colonial village of Plymouth, Massachusetts. He is eagerly awaiting his first opportunity to become a man by helping his father with the rye harvest.

Follow Samuel through his busy day as he awakes in the morning, dresses for the day, tends to his chores and accompanies his father to help with the rye harvest.

Meet the rest of his family—his father's new wife, Mam, and his younger sister Rachel. Follow them to the beach where they gather mussels for supper. Spend an evening of quiet recreation at home until Samuel falls asleep exhausted from his labors, but proud of his accomplishments and his father's encouraging words.

SAMUEL EATON'S DAY

SUMMARY OF RESPONSE:
Examine photographs from the literature selection and predict the story line and outcome prior to reading the story.

OBJECTIVE:
- The student will examine the photographs from the literature selection in order to predict story line, characters, setting and time period.
- The student will compare predictions with actual content.

THINKING LEVEL:
- Analysis

- Comprehension

MATERIALS:
- Literature selection
- Chart paper
- Marking pen
- Tape

PREPARATION:
- Tape the chart paper to the classroom wall.
- Select a student recorder.
- Gather in a cooperative group so all will have a clear view of the literature selection.

RESPONSE INSTRUCTIONS:
Begin this pre-reading strategy by sharing the literature selection with the students. Begin with the first page of the story and ask them to offer suggestions as to what they think the story is about. After several suggestions relating to one page are made, ask someone to make a summarizing statement. Are all in agreement? Record this statement on the chart paper. Continue to look through the literature selection and examine the photographs to determine what is happening in each picture. Write predictions based only on the pictures.

Read the book aloud to confirm or correct the story predictions recorded on the chart paper.

EVALUATION:
Is the student able to make content, character and time period predictions based on an examination of photographs? Can a comparison be made with actual content?

Respond

SAMUEL EATON'S DAY

SUMMARY OF RESPONSE:
Create a photo essay similar to the format of the literature selection and create a story to accompany it.

OBJECTIVE:
• The student will use photographs to tell a story.
• The student will use descriptive language to relate the story told by the photographs.

THINKING LEVEL:
• Synthesis
• Application

MATERIALS:
• Construction paper
• Paste, glue sticks
• Scissors
• Personal photographs, supplied by students

PREPARATION:
• Set up a table with art supplies. Vary the colors of construction paper from which students can choose.
• Ask students in advance to gather personal photographs to bring to class.

RESPONSE INSTRUCTIONS:
Examine the literature selection. Recall the pre-reading strategy used in Response #1. Could the story have been told using only pictures and eliminating text?

Ask students to use personal photographs to tell a story about an event in their life. Arrange the photographs on a construction paper background and glue or paste in place.

When the photo essays are complete, invite students to relate the story they think is conveyed by a classmate's pictures. The student who created the photo essay may evaluate how closely the interpretation comes to the actual story being told.

EVALUATION:
Is the student able to convey a story in a photo essay format? Is the student able to create a logical story by viewing a photo essay?

Respond

SAMUEL EATON'S DAY

SUMMARY OF RESPONSE:
Complete a Venn diagram comparing various aspects of childhood in colonial America and present-day America.

OBJECTIVE:
- The student will understand the concept of a Venn diagram.
- The student will draw comparisons between information from story content and personal knowledge.
- The student will present comparisons in a Venn diagram.

THINKING LEVEL:
- Comprehension
- Application
- Synthesis

MATERIALS:
- Butcher paper or chart paper
- Chalkboard
- Chalk
- Marking pens

PREPARATION:
- Introduce and explain a Venn diagram.
- Divide the class into cooperative groups.
- Assign a topic to each group (see below).
- Provide each group with chart paper and a marking pen.

RESPONSE INSTRUCTIONS:

Draw a Venn diagram on the chalkboard. Label the parts as shown at right. Explain its function. Choose one of the topics below to complete the sample diagram.

Each cooperative group focuses on the topic they are assigned. They brainstorm ideas about how aspects of colonial life differ from present-day. When the brainstorming is complete, the information gathered should be transferred to a Venn diagram on their chart paper. Topics to diagram include:

- *Chores*
- *Houses*
- *Tools*
- *Food*
- *Clothing*
- *Recreation*
- *Hunting*
- *Manners*

Display and discuss the diagram results.

Colonial Days

Both

Present Day

EVALUATION:
Can students use a Venn diagram to compare various aspects of a child living in colonial America and children at the present time?

Respond

SAMUEL EATON'S DAY

SUMMARY OF RESPONSE:
Work in pairs to complete a vocabulary map that defines, categorizes and establishes associations for words chosen from story content.

OBJECTIVE:
- The student will define vocabulary words from story content.
- The student will demonstrate knowledge of a vocabulary map.
- The student will identify word relationships.

THINKING LEVEL:
- Knowledge
- Comprehension
- Analysis

MATERIALS:
- Vocabulary map, following
- Glossary from literature selection
- Plain paper
- Pencils
- Chalkboard
- Chalk

PREPARATION:
- Divide into cooperative pairs.
- Reproduce a vocabulary map for each pair.
- Copy the sample below onto the chalkboard. Review the map with the students.
- Discuss the purpose of the *glossary* in the back of the literature selection.

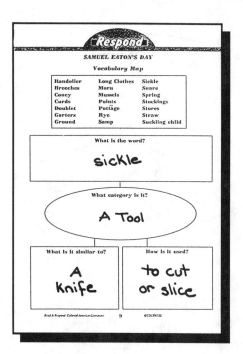

RESPONSE INSTRUCTIONS:
Introduce the vocabulary map to the students by displaying the example at left on the board and describing it.

When understanding is demonstrated, ask the partners to work together to create a map for each word in the box on their vocabulary map form. They will need extra paper for this purpose.

Share and compare results with the class by asking several students at a time to recreate the same vocabulary map on the chalkboard.

EVALUATION:
Can students use a vocabulary map to define given vocabulary words? Is the student able to break a word down into categories and associations?

SAMUEL EATON'S DAY

Vocabulary Map

Bandolier	Long Clothes	Sickle
Breeches	Morn	Snare
Coney	Mussels	Spring
Curds	Points	Stockings
Doublet	Pottage	Stores
Garters	Rye	Straw
Ground	Samp	Suckling child

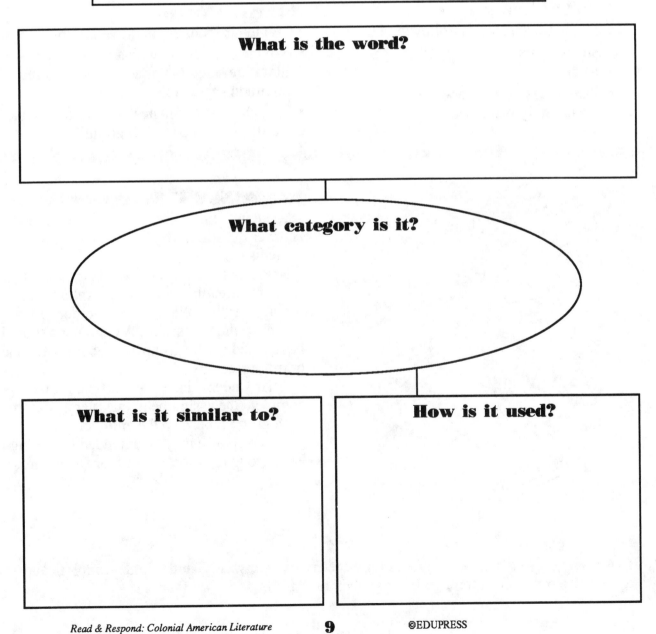

What is the word?

What category is it?

What is it similar to?

How is it used?

Respond

SAMUEL EATON'S DAY

SUMMARY OF RESPONSE:
Work in cooperative groups to complete task cards that require rereading with a focus for more critical analysis of story content.

OBJECTIVE:
- The student will recall facts, terms and basic content of the literature selection.
- The student will apply facts and terms to focused questions.
- The student will explore ideas through group collaboration.

THINKING LEVEL:
- Knowledge
- Application
- Synthesis

MATERIALS:
- Reading Focus Cards, following
- Paper
- Pencils
- Four copies of the literature selection, if available.

PREPARATION:
- Divide into four cooperative groups.
- Provide each group with a copy of the literature selection or access to one on a common share table.
- Cut apart and laminate the Reading Focus Cards. Give one to each group.

RESPONSE INSTRUCTIONS:
Review the purpose of each focus card. Answer questions about procedure that students may have.

Students focus on story content, either by recall or rereading story text. Explore ideas through group collaboration in order to complete the focus card. A consensus should be reached by the group and recorded by one or more students.

After students have had sufficient time to complete the assignment, one member from each group reports to the entire class.

This response may be extended by asking each group to complete all four focus cards.

EVALUATION:
Is the student able to read with a focus for more critical analysis? Can the student explore and expand on story content through group collaboration?

SAMUEL EATON'S DAY

Reading Focus Cards

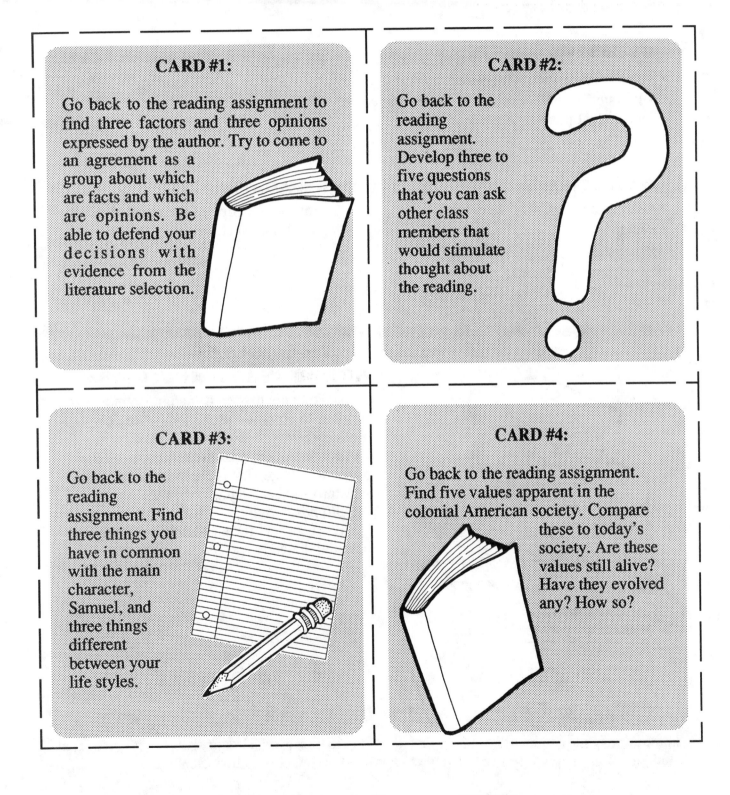

CARD #1:

Go back to the reading assignment to find three factors and three opinions expressed by the author. Try to come to an agreement as a group about which are facts and which are opinions. Be able to defend your decisions with evidence from the literature selection.

CARD #2:

Go back to the reading assignment. Develop three to five questions that you can ask other class members that would stimulate thought about the reading.

CARD #3:

Go back to the reading assignment. Find three things you have in common with the main character, Samuel, and three things different between your life styles.

CARD #4:

Go back to the reading assignment. Find five values apparent in the colonial American society. Compare these to today's society. Are these values still alive? Have they evolved any? How so?

Respond

SAMUEL EATON'S DAY

SUMMARY OF RESPONSE:

Complete a translation activity that demonstrates the understanding of dialect related to a historical era and group.

OBJECTIVE:

- The student will identify historic dialect.
- The student will develop responses that convey the meaning of dialect phrases in modern language.

THINKING LEVEL:

- Knowledge
- Application

MATERIALS:

- Translation activity page, following.
- Pencils

PREPARATION:

- Reproduce a copy of the translation activity page for each student.

RESPONSE INSTRUCTIONS:

Ask students to identify language that is not familiar to common usage today. Review the glossary terms.

Ask students to read the sentences on the translation page. Translate these sentences into familiar language.

Optional Activity:

- Write and perform a short play using colonial dialect.

EVALUATION:

Is the student able to identify dialect that is related to a historical era or specific group? Is the student able to apply familiar language to convey the meaning of historical dialect?

SAMUEL EATON'S DAY

Translate these sentences into familiar language.

1. I was a mere suckling child.

_____

2. I am up at first light.

_____

3. Thou must tend to thy labors before thou goest to the fields.

_____

4. I am afeared of being gammy at the work.

_____

5. Rachel is learning to eat upgrown food.

_____

6. We will have naught to eat this winter if we are slack and let the birds or the rains spoil the grain.

_____

7. I'll say narry a word.

_____

8. Dost think thou canst keep at the harvest with the upgrown people?

_____

9. Art thou faring well? Be thou too done to remain?

_____

10. He shows me how to hone the sickle.

_____

11. Tis but folly to spend time in bootless complaints.

_____

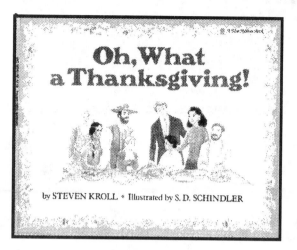

OH, WHAT A THANKSGIVING!

by Steven Kroll
Published by Scholastic Inc., 1988.
Canadian distribution by Scholastic, Canada.

DESCRIPTION:	**READING LEVEL:**
32 pages	Read aloud—Grades 1-2
Picture book	Independent—Grades 3-6

CONTENT NOTES:

This Blue Ribbon Book compares the differences between life today and life in colonial days. David, the main character in the story, uses his imagination to travel back in time to experience one of the first Thanksgiving meals. Many modern conveniences and luxuries are displayed in the illustrations with a drastic comparison of the difficulty of survival that people had to face in colonial days.

CONTENT SUMMARY:

While celebrating present day Thanksgiving, David is intrigued by the Thanksgivings of the past. He travels back and forth, imagining himself and his family in colonial times. As he rides home on the school bus he imagines that he is on the *Mayflower* crossing the great Atlantic Ocean. David wants to hunt for the Thanksgiving meal and eat exactly what the Pilgrims ate at their meal. His father and mother do not seem to join in the spirit of David's adventure, but his teacher helps him to understand that he should be thankful for how tradition has evolved because today's celebration is every Pilgrim boy's dream. David realizes that he has as many things to be thankful for as the Pilgrims did centuries ago.

OH, WHAT A THANKSGIVING!

SUMMARY OF RESPONSE:
Conduct a research activity that gathers information about what was eaten at the first Thanksgiving meal.

OBJECTIVE:
- The student will use research techniques to gather information.
- The student will defend his/her findings with facts gained from research.

THINKING LEVEL:
- Knowledge
- Synthesis

MATERIALS:
- Research books
- Paper
- Pencil
- Chart paper
- Marking pens

PREPARATION:
- Gather research books or schedule your class to meet in the library.
- Divide into small cooperative groups.
- Provide each group with chart paper and a marking pen.

RESPONSE INSTRUCTIONS:
Work individually to gather information about food that was believed to have been eaten at the first Thanksgiving celebration. When the information-gathering period is over, compare notes with the rest of the students in the cooperative group. Compile conclusions and record them on the chart paper.

Ask a student moderator to share the group's conclusions with the remainder of the class.

EVALUATION:
Is the student able to use research resources to find answers to a focused question? Is the student able to draw conclusions based on gathered information?

Respond

OH, WHAT A THANKSGIVING!

SUMMARY OF RESPONSE:
Complete a chart that compares and contrasts the first Thanksgiving with present Thanksgiving celebrations.

OBJECTIVE:
- The student will notice the similarities and differences between present-day Thanksgiving and that of the past.
- The students will organize their findings and display them in a comparison chart.

THINKING LEVEL:
- Comprehension
- Application

MATERIALS:
- Comparison chart, following
- Pen or pencil

PREPARATION:
- Reproduce and distribute one copy of the comparison chart to each student.

RESPONSE INSTRUCTIONS:
Review the comparison chart with the students. Ask them to think about each category on the chart as it relates to their personal Thanksgiving celebration. Write the responses in the **My Thanksgiving** column on the chart. Complete the chart by restating information from the literature selection in the **First Thanksgiving** column.

Gather together for a cooperative discussion that compares and contrasts the information on the completed charts.

EVALUATION:
Is the student able to complete a chart that reflects information from both reading content and personal experience? Is the student able to draw conclusions based on the information?

OH, WHAT A THANKSGIVING!

	MY THANKSGIVING	FIRST THANKSGIVING
Guests		
Chores		
Food		
Clothing		
Activities		
Things To Be Thankful For		

OH, WHAT A THANKSGIVING!

SUMMARY OF RESPONSE:
Create a wardrobe for paper dolls that is historically accurate in depicting clothing worn during the colonial era.

OBJECTIVE:
- The student will research and identify by name, clothing worn by boys and girls during colonial times.
- The student will demonstrate this knowledge by creating a paper doll wardrobe.

THINKING LEVEL:
- Knowledge
- Application

MATERIALS:
- Paper doll patterns, following
- Assorted scraps of fabric or paper
- Resource books that illustrate clothing worn during the colonial period
- Poster board   • Scissors
- Glue   • Crayons

PREPARATION:
- Arrange books on a cooperative-use table.
- Reproduce a copy of the boy and girl paper dolls for each student.
- Provide each student with a piece of poster board the size of the two dolls.

RESPONSE INSTRUCTIONS:
After researching the clothing of the boys and the girls in colonial days, students design authentic clothing for their paper dolls. The dolls should first be cut out and mounted on sturdy backing such as cardboard or poster board. Clothing may be made from paper or fabric.

Students should be prepared to recall the colonial name and relate information about each article of clothing.

Optional activity: Make a cooperative mural that illustrates and labels colonial clothing such as breeches, doublet and falling band.

EVALUATION:
Can the student recall the original names for the articles of clothing? Are they able to dress the paper dolls in clothing typical for the colonial era?

OH, WHAT A THANKSGIVING!

OH, WHAT A THANKSGIVING!

SUMMARY OF RESPONSE:
Design and write an invitation to a colonial-day Pilgrim or Native American asking them to visit and celebrate a present-day Thanksgiving. Follow with a perspective discussion.

OBJECTIVE:
- The student will write in the form of an invitation.
- The student will relate observations based on another's viewpoint.

THINKING LEVEL:
- Application
- Application

MATERIALS:
- Paper
- Pencil
- Crayons
- Samples of party or event invitations

PREPARATION:
- Share samples of invitations with students.

RESPONSE INSTRUCTIONS:
Make a list of the important elements to include in the invitation to your colonial-era guest. Include such information as time, date, what to wear, place, what to bring, how to dress. Design and write an original invitation.

Follow with a group discussion from the viewpoint of the invited guest. Consider:
- What changes would be the most surprising for the visitor?
- What might be the most enjoyable part of their experience?
- What might be the most uncomfortable part of their experience?
- Would the Native American be more comfortable than the colonial guest?

EVALUATION:
Is the student able to recognize the differences in the Thanksgiving celebration of long ago and now? Can the student identify the changes that would surprise the Indians or Pilgrims?

Respond

OH, WHAT A THANKSGIVING!

SUMMARY OF RESPONSE:
Investigate and develop a time line that shows how the first Thanksgiving was celebrated and how the celebration has progressed over the years to its present-day form.

OBJECTIVE:
- The student will explore the history of the Thanksgiving holiday to determine changes in the celebration.
- The student will develop a time line that illustrates the research conclusions.

THINKING LEVEL:
- Analysis
- Application

MATERIALS:
- Reference books
- Roll of paper
- Markers, paint, crayons, paper, glue and other art supplies

PREPARATION:
- Arrange the reference books and art materials on a cooperative-use table.
- Divide the class into groups of four to six students.
- Provide each group with butcher paper long enough to create a time line.

RESPONSE INSTRUCTIONS:
Select a recorder, line drawer, measurer and writer within each cooperative group (more than one student may have the same job). All students work together to locate facts and information about changes in the traditions of the Thanksgiving holiday celebration. The recorder writes the information.

When the facts have been gathered, the students decide on an art medium to use to depict this information in a time line mural. The line drawer will create the line that indicates dates and the passing of time. The measurer will help the line drawer space the dates to accurately reflect the passage of time between each change. The recorder and writer will work together to transfer information to the time line. All students will participate in the illustration of the time line. Each group may present their time line. Discussion and comparisons may follow.

Optional activity: For an additional challenge, have students discuss the connection between the changes and what was going on in society at the time.

EVALUATION:
Are the students able to depict changes in the Thanksgiving celebration in a time line format? Can they make a connection between societal changes and the holiday's customs?

OH, WHAT A THANKSGIVING!

SUMMARY OF RESPONSE:
Select a famous colonial American to research and impersonate in a speech.

OBJECTIVE:
- The student will identify and conduct research about a famous colonial American.
- The students will compile facts to use in the creation of a speech.

THINKING LEVEL:
- Application
- Synthesis

MATERIALS:
- Research books
- Speech Planner, following
- Dramatic play props and costumes (student supplied)
- Index cards

PREPARATION:
- Place research books on a group-use table.
- Invite a guest to present an impersonation speech as a model for student speeches.
- Reproduce and distribute a copy of the Speech Planner and several index cards to each student.

RESPONSE INSTRUCTIONS:
Each student selects one of the famous colonial Americans mentioned in the literature selection to read about and research. These include: Captain Miles Standish, Governor Bradford, Chief Massasoit, Samoset, Squanto.

Students complete the questions on the Speech Planner as a guide to research. When all questions are answered, the information is transferred to a speech format. Notes for the speech may be prepared on index cards.

Each student is responsible for assembling any props or costumes he or she will present and wear during the impersonation speech.

Classmates may ask the speaker additional questions. The speaker should remain in role while answering questions.

EVALUATION:
Is the student able to gather relevant and accurate facts about the colonial American? Is the student able to transfer information to a speech format?

OH, WHAT A THANKSGIVING!
Colonial American Speech Planner

1. What is the name of the person? Where and when did this person live?

2. What was this person's heritage?

3. What other significant events happened in his lifetime?

4. Who were his friends? his enemies?

5. How would his personality be described?

6. What did he look like?

7. How did this person make our country a better place in which to live?

8. What do you feel would impress him the most about our country today?

9. Why was he mentioned in this book?

10. If he were alive today, what would you ask him about?

... *IF YOU LIVED IN COLONIAL TIMES*
by Ann McGovern
Published by Scholastic, Inc., 1992.
Canadian distribution by Scholastic, Canada.

DESCRIPTION:
80 pages
Informative text

READING LEVEL:
Read aloud—Grades 2
Independent—Grades 3-6

CONTENT NOTES:

The text does not include information about all thirteen colonial colonies, only the New England colonies that later became Connecticut, Rhode Island, Massachusetts, New Hampshire, Vermont and Maine. Its question-answer format presents facts in an easy-to-understand way for younger readers. Scholastic also publishes other books in this series that tell how children lived long ago. The table of contents serves as a quick planning and information guide.

CONTENT SUMMARY:

This book tells you what it was like to be a boy or girl in the New England colonies during the years 1630 to 1730. A wide variety of questions about colonial life are asked and answered. Find out basic information about what people were like, what they ate and how they dressed. Learn about other facets of colonial life such as customs, terminology, transportation and traditions. Discover unusual facts about recreation, school, community, punishment and laws. There is also detailed information about the occupations in a colonial town including cobblers, hatters, blacksmiths, silversmiths, tinsmiths, tanners, coopers, cabinetmakers and tailors.

... IF YOU LIVED IN COLONIAL TIMES

SUMMARY OF RESPONSE:

Participate in a pre-reading strategy by creating and completing a **KWL** chart (Know, Want To Know, Learned) about the colonial days.

OBJECTIVE:

- The student will answer the questions based on previously-known information.
- The student will find facts about a focused topic.
- The student will compare and determine accuracy of previously-learned information.

THINKING LEVEL:

- Knowledge

- Comprehension
- Evaluation

MATERIALS:

- Overhead projector
- Overhead transparency
- Chart paper
- Marking pen

PREPARATION:

- Reproduce the table of contents from the literature selection on transparency film.
- Prepare chart paper by marking columns labeled: **Know, Want To Know, Learned**.

RESPONSE INSTRUCTIONS:

Place the table of contents transparency on the overhead projector. Students read the table of contents and indicate those questions to which they think they know the answers. Record the answers in the **Know** column on the chart paper.

Next, students indicate areas of interest in the table of contents. List these in the **Want To Know** column. Divide into similar interest groups and assign that part of the text to each group for further investigation. After fact gathering is complete, the groups teach the rest of the class what they learned. Record this information in the **Learned** column on the chart.

Compare **learned** information with the **know** information. How accurate was students' prior knowledge on the subject of colonial times?

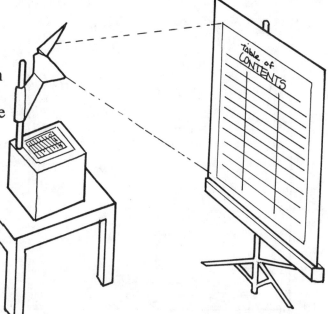

EVALUATION:

Is the student able to draw on previously-learned knowledge? Is the student able to conduct research with a focus? Does the student exhibit understanding of a KWL chart?

Respond

... IF YOU LIVED IN COLONIAL TIMES

SUMMARY OF RESPONSE:
Design a poster that reflects knowledge and comprehension about law, crime and punishment during colonial times.

OBJECTIVE:
• The student will recall several laws used and enacted during colonial times.
• The student will explain why these laws were enforced.
• The student will determine an appropriate punishment for breaking a law.

THINKING LEVEL:
• Knowledge

• Comprehension
• Application

MATERIALS:
• Town Notice poster, following
• Pencil
• Crayons

PREPARATION:
• Review the chapters in the literature selection that focus on laws.
• Reproduce the Town Notice for each student.
• Review the Town Notice and answer any questions students may have about how to complete it.

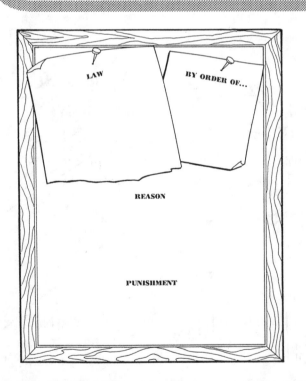

RESPONSE INSTRUCTIONS:
Students review the chapters in the literature selection that provide information about laws and punishment during colonial times.
When facts have been gathered, each student completes all the sections in the Town Notice.
• **Law:** Clearly state the law in force.
• **By order of:** Who was responsible for enacting this law?
• **Reason:** Who might have originated this law and way was it written?
• **Punishment:** What is the punishment for anyone breaking the law?
Color the Town Notice border and post all on a community bulletin board. Ask a *town crier* to announce and inform all colonial classroom citizens of the laws.

EVALUATION:
Is the student able to recall laws and tell the reason why they were enacted? Can the student determine originator and appropriate punishment for laws during colonial times?

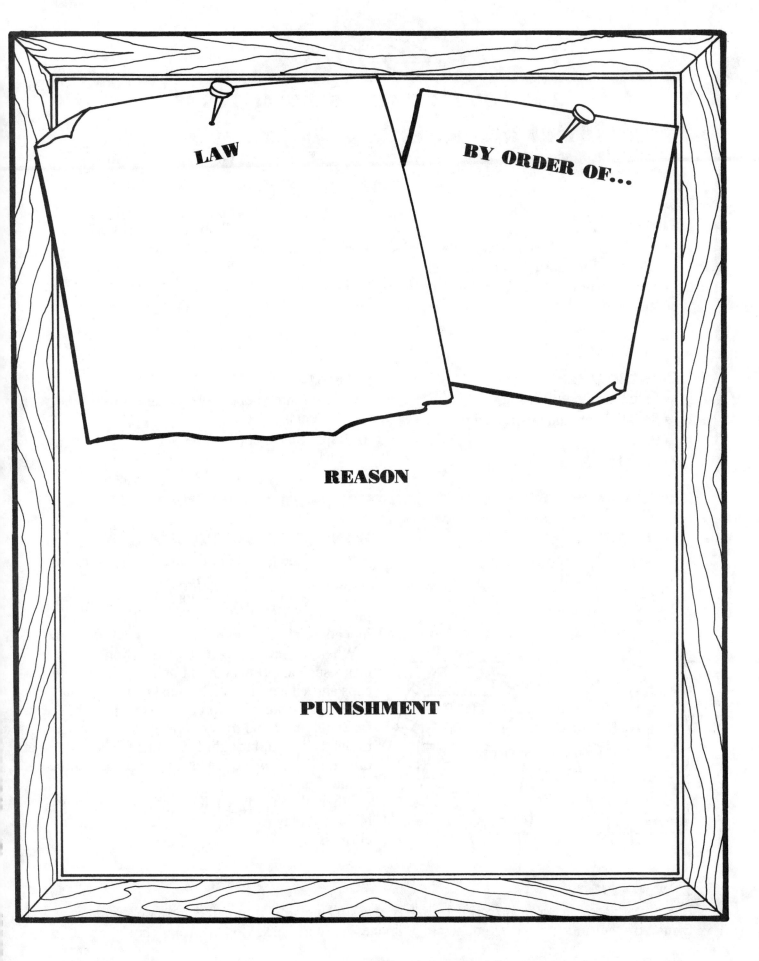

... IF YOU LIVED IN COLONIAL TIMES

SUMMARY OF RESPONSE:
Write a script and present a short play, complete with props, that reenacts the childhood school experience during colonial times.

OBJECTIVE:
- The student will relate information gained from content about school during colonial times.
- The student will write and present a dramatization of colonial school life.

THINKING LEVEL:
- Knowledge
- Synthesis

MATERIALS:
- Script Guide, following
- Supplies for student-created props
- Paper
- Pencil

PREPARATION:
- Divide into cooperative groups of 6-8 students.
- Reproduce a copy of the Script Guide for each group.
- Select a producer and director in each group.

RESPONSE INSTRUCTIONS:
Review the Script Guide and the elements in writing a script with the students.

Each group uses the Script Guide to help produce a script that accurately reflects events in a colonial classroom.

When the script is complete, decisions for props such as primers, hornbooks, quills, dunce caps and whispering sticks must be made and the props created. The producer is responsible for seeing to it that material needs are indicated to the teacher or brought from home. The director oversees the rehearsal and presentation of the skit.

When all is ready, each group performs their historical play for classmates, parents or other classes.

EVALUATION:
Is the student able write in script form? Is the student able to conduct research with a focus? Are the students able to cooperate with one another in order to perform a play?

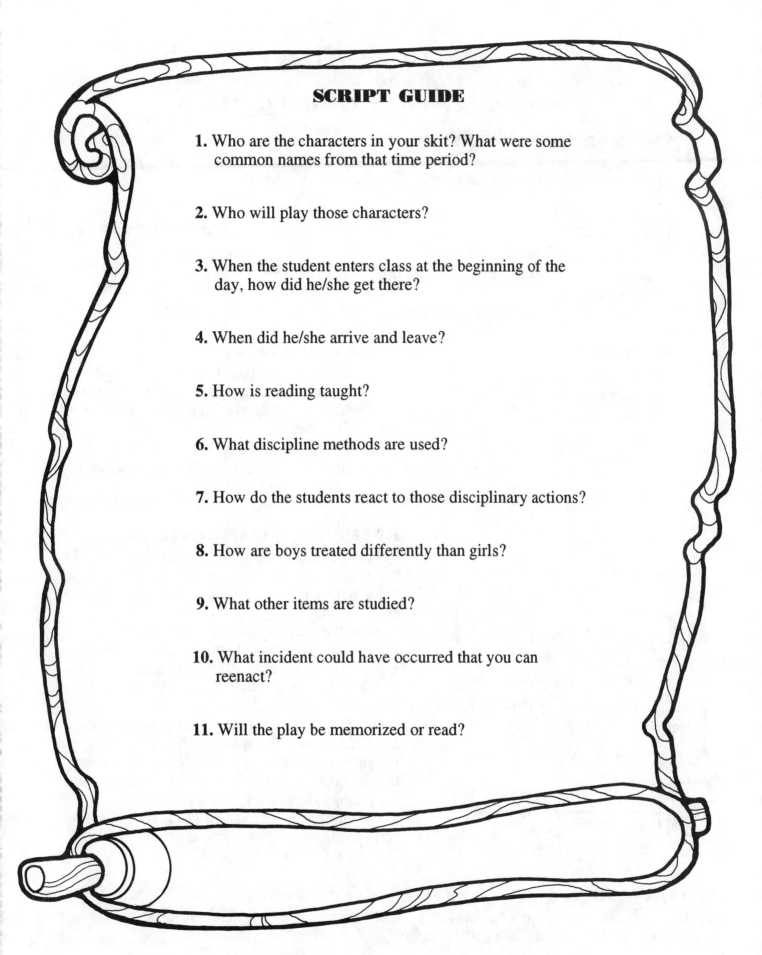

SCRIPT GUIDE

1. Who are the characters in your skit? What were some common names from that time period?

2. Who will play those characters?

3. When the student enters class at the beginning of the day, how did he/she get there?

4. When did he/she arrive and leave?

5. How is reading taught?

6. What discipline methods are used?

7. How do the students react to those disciplinary actions?

8. How are boys treated differently than girls?

9. What other items are studied?

10. What incident could have occurred that you can reenact?

11. Will the play be memorized or read?

... IF YOU LIVED IN COLONIAL TIMES

SUMMARY OF RESPONSE:
Develop and play a question-and-answer game, similar to the television game show, Jeopardy, based on the table of contents in the literature selection.

OBJECTIVE:
- The student will read and use a table of contents.
- The student will formulate and answer questions based on reading content.
- The student will develop a game based on story content.

THINKING LEVEL:
- Knowledge
- Comprehension
- Synthesis

MATERIALS:
- Poster board
- Library book pockets
- Index cards
- Rubber cement
- Marking pen

PREPARATION:
- Make a game board by attaching book pockets to poster board with rubber cement Assign points to each pocket (see illustration).
- Have a copy of the table of contents from the literature selection available for student review.

RESPONSE INSTRUCTIONS:

Students select one question from the Table of Contents to answer. There should be no repetition. Some may need to select more than one in order to cover all chapters.

Write the question on one side of the index card and the answer on the other. Place a card, answer side out, in each pocket. Try to place the card in a pocket with a point value that matches the difficulty of the question.

Divide into several teams. One person at a time from each team participates. Select a card and read the answer. The first person to respond with the correct question from the Table of Contents scores the points indicated on the pocket.

The team with the most points at the end of a predetermined length of time is given the title of "Colonial Experts".

EVALUATION:
Is the student able to match answers to questions based on story content? Is the student able to use a table of contents as a guide to locating information?

... IF YOU LIVED IN COLONIAL TIMES

SUMMARY OF RESPONSE:
Create a stitchery or clothing-related project using colonial methods.

OBJECTIVE:
- The student will take part in a colonial-based sewing activity.
- The student will compare differences in modern-day versus colonial-era clothing manufacturing.

THINKING LEVEL:
- Application
- Evaluation

MATERIALS:
- Weaving loom
- Flowers, berries or roots for dying (or fabric dye)
- Pot
- Hot plate
- Embroidery needles
- Knitting needles
- Yarn
- Thread
- Colored floss
- Fabric scraps

PREPARATION:
- Set up centers for each of the suggested activities below.
- Arrange for parent volunteers to assist students in each center.
- Divide into activity-interest groups so that the correct amount of materials can be gathered ahead of time.

RESPONSE INSTRUCTIONS:
Students divide into the various groups depending on the interest area selected and report to the appropriate classroom station.
- Create a weaving from strips of fabric
- Dye fabric using flowers, berries or roots
- Stitch a sampler with a motto
- Make a doll from rags
- Learn to knit

Parents assist at each station to ensure student safety and success. If time permits, several stations can be visited. The students will discuss their experience and make comparisons with modern-day techniques.

EVALUATION:
Is the student able to demonstrate a process involved in making colonial-era projects? Is the student able to draw comparisons between modern and colonial era methods?

... IF YOU LIVED IN COLONIAL TIMES

SUMMARY OF RESPONSE:
Investigate and write job description cards for colonial occupations to use in a cooperative game of charades.

OBJECTIVE:
- The student will identify colonial-era occupations.
- The student will describe an occupation by summarizing information.
- The student will, through dramatic play, convey the concept of an occupation.

THINKING LEVEL:
- Recall
- Comprehension
- Application

MATERIALS:
- Occupation Cards, following
- Scissors   • Index cards
- Pencils   • Stapler
- Paper bag

PREPARATION:
- Cut apart the occupation cards.
- Staple each one to an index card.
- Give an index card to each student.

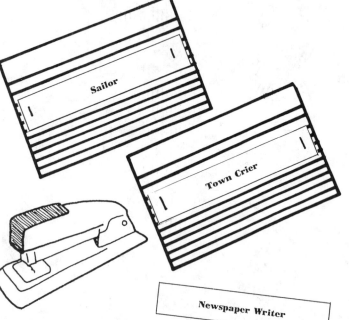

RESPONSE INSTRUCTIONS:
A variety of jobs were essential in the colonial community. Many are listed on the Occupation Cards on the following page.

Each student investigates the occupation on the card they received (see Preparation). They write a job description for that occupation on the index card.

Place all index cards in a paper bag. Play a game of charades. Ask a student to draw a card out of the bag and act out the occupation. No words may be used, only actions. Classmates try to guess which occupation is being portrayed.

EVALUATION:
Can the student summarize an occupation with historical accuracy? Is the student able to effectively portray an occupation in a game of charades?

... IF YOU LIVED IN COLONIAL TIMES

Sailor	Clockmaker
Town Crier	Miller
Post Rider	Wheelwright
Newspaper Writer	Cooper
Teacher	Barber
Medicine Seller	Tailor
Town Watchman	Tinsmith
Minister	Shipbuilder
Blacksmith	Farmer
Pewterer	Hunter
Tanner	Cook
Silversmith	Fisherman
Cabinetmaker	Butcher

THE MATCHLOCK GUN
by Walter D. Edmonds
Published by G.P. Putnam's Sons, 1941 and 1969.
Canadian distribution by Vanwell Publishing.

DESCRIPTION:
50 pages
Picture book with chapters

READING LEVEL:
Read aloud—Grades 3-4
Independent—Grades 5-6

CONTENT NOTES:

The Matchlock Gun was awarded the Newbery Medal in 1942 as "the most distinguished contribution to American literature for children." Its setting, the Hudson Valley in colonial New York, is a favorite of the author's. The characters and events depicted are based on actual people and occurrences. Trudy, who learned to spin at the age of six due to her mother's crippling injury, became so well-known for her spinning abilities that her story has been told from generation to generation.

CONTENT SUMMARY:

The Van Alstyne family, Teunis, Gertrude and their children Edward and Trudy, came to America from Germany and settled in the Hudson Valley around Albany, New York, when New York was still a British colony. The French were leading the Indians in raids against the colonists and Teunis, a captain in the militia, was often called away from home to help defend the region from the assaults.

It was during one of these times that the Indians evaded the militia and attacked the colonists. Ten-year-old Edward had been shown how to use the matchlock gun that hangs over the fireplace. In a daring plan to protect her family against the Indians, Gertrude lures them to her home, hoping that the instructions she gave Edward will be listened to and followed and save them all from certain death.

THE MATCHLOCK GUN

SUMMARY OF RESPONSE:
Conduct a mock trial that puts students in the position of defending or prosecuting Edward for his role in the death of the Indian.

OBJECTIVE:
• The students will understand the role of the participants and terms used in a trial.
• The student will support a position with logical arguments in the form of a mock trial.

THINKING LEVEL:
• Comprehension

• Synthesis

MATERIALS:
• Newspaper articles about current trials
• Resource books or movies about courtroom people and procedures
• Gavel

PREPARATION:
• Arrange the classroom to resemble a courtroom.
• Appoint a judge and jury then divide the rest of the class into two teams.
• Discuss the elements of a trial.

RESPONSE INSTRUCTIONS:
Is Edward guilty or innocent in the death of the Indian who attacked his home and his family? This is the issue on trial in the classroom courtroom.

Acquaint students with courtroom terms, people and procedures. Allow defense and prosecution teams time to prepare their case. When ready, the members present logical arguments to the judge and jury.

The jury discusses the cases presented and issues a verdict. What arguments influenced their decision the most and why?

Optional activity: Look for current events or information about trials in the news. Are any of them similar to the case in your classroom courtroom?

EVALUATION:
Can the student give relevant facts regarding their side of the issue? Is the student able to identify words related to the courtroom? Can comparisons be drawn with current issues?

THE MATCHLOCK GUN

SUMMARY OF RESPONSE:
Locate context clues that indicate the Van Alstyne family chores then churn butter from milk to put on top of johnnycakes.

OBJECTIVE:
- The student will select context clues to answer a question.
- The students will identify the sequence in a colonial food-making process.
- The student will follow a recipe to complete a cooking project.

THINKING LEVEL:
- Knowledge
- Comprehension

- Comprehension

MATERIALS:
- Recipes, following
- Glass jar with lid
- Heavy whipping cream
- Egg   • Fork
- Griddle   • Bowl
- Spatula
- Cornmeal
- Salt
- Milk
- Large spoons
- Cooking oil
- Strainer

PREPARATION:
- Gather equipment used in the food-preparation process.
- Divide into four cooperative groups.
- Reproduce copies of the recipe page and distribute one to each group.

RESPONSE INSTRUCTIONS:
Begin with a whole-class activity by recalling context clues that tell about the chores the Van Alstyne family might have completed during the course of their day. Discuss the food they may have eaten at a meal or that Teunis may have taken with him when he traveled.

Review the recipes with each group. Each group member participates by helping with measuring, stirring, shaking the cream jar until it turns into butter, pouring the batter onto the griddle and serving the johnnycakes.

While enjoying the food, discuss the steps that a colonial cook would have taken to make the same recipe. How might it differ from their classroom cooking experience?

EVALUATION:
Does the student understand the concept of context clues? Can the student locate information by looking for context clues? Is the student able to follow directions to complete a recipe?

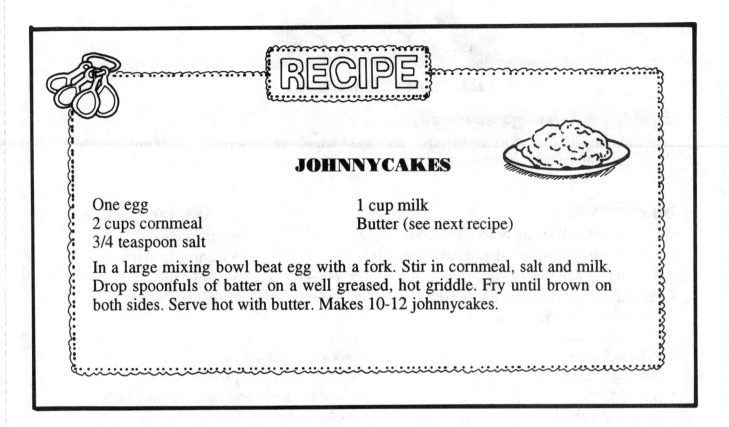

JOHNNYCAKES

One egg
2 cups cornmeal
3/4 teaspoon salt

1 cup milk
Butter (see next recipe)

In a large mixing bowl beat egg with a fork. Stir in cornmeal, salt and milk. Drop spoonfuls of batter on a well greased, hot griddle. Fry until brown on both sides. Serve hot with butter. Makes 10-12 johnnycakes.

BUTTER

Heavy whipping cream
Salt
Glass jar with lid

Fill jar half-full with heavy whipping cream that is room temperature. Shake jar until curd separates from the whey. Pour curd into a strainer to get excess liquid off. Add salt to butter to taste.

THE MATCHLOCK GUN

SUMMARY OF RESPONSE:
Use context clues to write descriptive paragraphs and create labeled diagrams of the matchlock gun in the literature selection.

OBJECTIVE:
• The student will locate descriptive context clues.
• The student will write a descriptive paragraph.
• The student will make estimations using context clues.
• The student will create a labeled diagram to match their estimations and descriptions.

THINKING LEVEL:
• Application
• Comprehension
• Application
• Evaluation

MATERIALS:
• Construction paper
• Crayons
• Paper and pencil
• Tape measure
• Scale

PREPARATION:
• Divide class into groups of four.
• Place the scale and tape measure on a cooperative-use table.
• Cut construction paper in half, lengthwise.

RESPONSE INSTRUCTIONS:
Work in cooperative groups to locate and list phrases in the literature selection that give clues as to the size, weight, length and appearance of the matchlock gun.

Incorporate the phrases to write a descriptive paragraph. Include detail about the matchlock gun not included in content, but that can be inferred through the context clues. Encourage students to use the scale and tape measure to help them with their estimations about size and weight. Students should be prepared to support estimations with content facts.

Draw an illustrative diagram of the matchlock gun based on the descriptive paragraphs. Label all parts. Include information about length and weight.

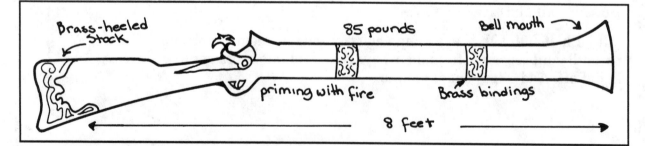

EVALUATION:
Can the student use context clues as guides to writing a descriptive paragraph? Is the student able to make inferences based on these clues? Does the student understand a diagram?

Respond

THE MATCHLOCK GUN

SUMMARY OF RESPONSE:
Brainstorm, develop and diagram an alternate plan that might save the family from the Indian attack.

OBJECTIVE:
- The student will identify the story's main problem and its solution.
- The student will brainstorm and develop an alternate solution to the one presented in story content.
- The student will present the solution in a labeled diagram that reflects knowledge of story setting and characters.

THINKING LEVEL:
- Knowledge
- Application
- Synthesis

MATERIALS:
- Writing paper or notebook
- Pencil
- Crayons
- Large sheet construction paper

PREPARATION:
- Review how the family handled the Indian attack in the literature selection.
- Form cooperative brainstorming groups.

RESPONSE INSTRUCTIONS:
The students brainstorm within their groups to propose alternative ways the family in the literature selection might have handled the problem of an Indian attack. Record all ideas for ten minutes. The group must select the one idea that appears to be the most viable. Discuss the idea in detail.

When the solution is determined, several in the group prepare an oral description of the alternate solution. The remaining group members draw a diagram that relates the sequence of the plan and labels all characters and setting details. The two presentations should be coordinated. Present both to classmates.

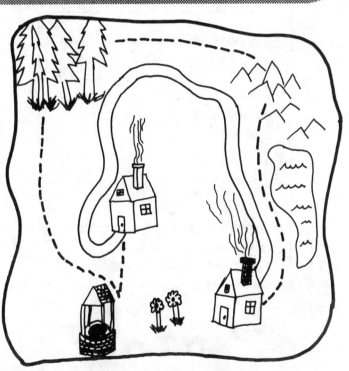

EVALUATION:
Are the students able to think of alternatives to a problem? Are they able to describe and diagram a solution in a clear manner? Are they able to judge the validity of their plan?

THE MATCHLOCK GUN

SUMMARY OF RESPONSE:
Write a letter from the perspective of the young boy in the story as he describes the Indian attack on their home.

OBJECTIVE:
- The student will write a letter in the style of the colonial days.
- The student will describe the events of the Indian attack from Edward's perspective.
- The student will infer emotional response based on content.

THINKING LEVEL:
- Application
- Application

- Evaluation

MATERIALS:
- Stationery page, following
- Blank envelopes
- Pencils
- Samples of letters and previously addressed envelopes

PREPARATION:
- Reproduce two copies of the stationery page for each student. Give each two envelopes.
- Review the chapter "How would you write a letter in colonial days?" from the book *If You Lived In Colonial Times*, if available.
- Share samples of letter and envelope format.

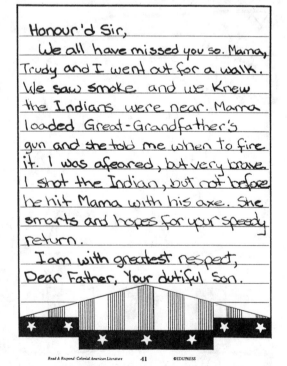

Honour'd Sir,
    We all have missed you so. Mama, Trudy and I went out for a walk. We saw smoke and we knew the Indians were near. Mama loaded Great-Grandfather's gun and she told me when to fire it. I was afeared, but very brave. I shot the Indian, but not before he hit Mama with his axe. She smarts and hopes for your speedy return.
    I am with greatest respect, Dear Father, Your dutiful Son.

Read & Respond: Colonial American Literature   41   ©EDUPRESS

RESPONSE INSTRUCTIONS:
Students pretend that they are Edward writing a letter to his father. The letter must begin with Dear Sir or Honour'd Sir. It will explain what happened during the Indian attack on their home while the father was away. It should also include thoughts about Edward's emotions during and after the attack. End the letter with an appropriate colonial closing such as, "I am with greatest respect, Dear Father, Your dutiful Son".

Address an envelope and "mail" it to another student in class. That student opens and reads the letter then writes a response letter from Sam's father to Sam on the second sheet of stationery. Address an envelope to Sam and "mail" it back to the original student.

EVALUATION:
Is the student able to describe the events of the attack in sequence? Are they able to write from the perspective of Edward? Is the student able to infer emotion from story context?

THE MATCHLOCK GUN

SUMMARY OF RESPONSE:
Work in pairs to classify the main characters' personality traits then use this information to make predictions about the characters' actions in a present-day situation.

OBJECTIVE:
- The student will classify the main characters' personalities by examining their actions in the story.
- The student will consider the personality traits in order to predict that character's actions in a present-day situation.

THINKING LEVEL:
- Analysis
- Synthesis

MATERIALS:
- Character Predictions, following
- Pencils
- Chalk
- Chalkboard

PREPARATION:
- Divide into groups of four students.
- List the four main characters—Teunis, Gertrude, Edward, Trudy—on the chalkboard.
- Reproduce four pages of the Character Predictions for each group.

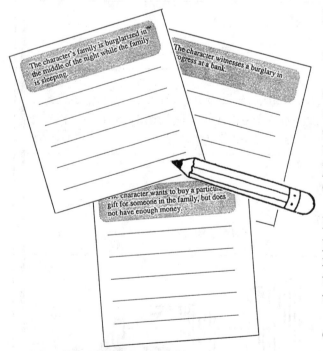

RESPONSE INSTRUCTIONS:
As a class, brainstorm personality traits. List them on the chalkboard. Each one may be discussed briefly.

When the list is complete, work in smaller groups to classify each main character's personality traits based on his or her actions in context. Use the list on the chalkboard for assistance. Write the associated traits under the character's name at the top of the prediction page. Be prepared to provide evidence from story content to support the decision.

When the list is complete, read the present-day hypothetical situation in each box on the prediction page. Predict the action the character in consideration might take in that situation, based on the personality traits that have been identified. Write the consensus in the space provided.

Complete a prediction page for each character. Gather as a group and compare responses.

EVALUATION:
Is the student able to accurately describe the character from the context clues? Can the students make predictions that apply these personality traits in a present-day situation?

THE MATCHLOCK GUN

Character Predictions

Character Name:

Personality Traits:

The character's family is burglarized in the middle of the night while the family is sleeping.

_____

_____

_____

_____

The character witnesses a burglary in progress at a bank.

_____

_____

_____

_____

The character must leave their family to travel alone to a foreign country.

_____

_____

_____

_____

The character wants to buy a particular gift for someone in the family, but does not have enough money.

_____

_____

_____

_____

A LION TO GUARD US

by Clyde Robert Bulla
Published by Harper Trophy, 1989.
Canadian distribution by HarperCollins.

DESCRIPTION:	READING LEVEL:
117 pages	Read aloud—Grades 3-4
Chapter book	Independent—Grades 5-6

CONTENT NOTES:

The historical note at the back of the literature selection points out many facts about the dangers settlers faced on the voyage across the ocean and the hardships that awaited them on their arrival in the newly-founded village of Jamestown. The historical note also retells the true story of the wreck of one ship that sailed from England in a fleet with eight others carrying help and supplies to the colonies—the story on which this historically-accurate novel is based.

CONTENT SUMMARY:

Living as a servant in a house of a stingy and mean-tempered mistresses, Amanda must work to feed her little brother and sister. Her mother has fallen very ill. Her father sailed away to the New World to help construct buildings in Virginia and has been gone for three years. Amanda's work is hard and, while she tries her best, she cannot forget her family's goal to join their father in the New World.

When Amanda's mother dies, Amanda is faced with what to do about her difficult situation. Being strong-willed, she quits her job in hope of sailing to the New World. The children depart with the protection of a brass lion's head given to them by their father. The challenges, heartache and fears of the journey are overshadowed when the children are rewarded by finding their father after arriving in Jamestown.

Respond

A LION TO GUARD US

SUMMARY OF RESPONSE:
Participate in a pre-reading strategy that makes predictions about story content based on the cover picture and literature title.

OBJECTIVE:
- The student will make predictions about story content by referring to the cover picture and story title.
- The student will determine the accuracy of these predictions after reading the literature selection.

THINKING LEVEL:
- Analysis
- Comprehension

MATERIALS:
- Paper
- Pencil
- Literature selection

PREPARATION:
- Distribute a paper and pencil to each student.
- Ask students to fold their paper in half. At the top of one column, write **Prediction**. At the top of the second column write **Result**.

RESPONSE INSTRUCTIONS:
This is a pre-reading strategy. Show the cover of the literature selection. Review the title. Have students speculate about the story. Who are the people on the cover? What is their relationship? What are they doing on the ship? Where are they going? What might the title have to do with story plot? Allow ten minutes for students to write their predictions in the correct column on their paper.

Cooperatively, share the individual predictions and the reasons behind them. Can the group reach a general consensus about the story line?

As the story is read, make notes about the accuracy of the predictions in the **Result** column of their pre-reading worksheets.

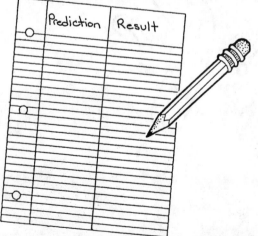

EVALUATION:
Can the student use the front picture and the title as a guide to predict what the story will be about? Can the student evaluate the accuracy of the predictions?

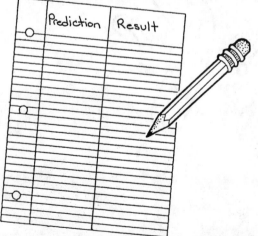

A LION TO GUARD US

SUMMARY OF RESPONSE:
Complete a character questionnaire in order to write a personality profile of one of the main characters in the story.

OBJECTIVE:
- The student will choose one of three characters.
- The student will answer the character questions in relation to the chosen character.
- The student will compile the answers to compose a character personality.

THINKING LEVEL:
- Knowledge
- Comprehension
- Synthesis

MATERIALS:
- Character Study Questionnaire, following
- Pencil or pen

PREPARATION:
- Reproduce the Character Study Questionnaire and distribute one to each student.

RESPONSE INSTRUCTIONS:
Review the Character Study Questionnaire with the students and answer any questions they may have. Ask students to choose either Mistress Trippet, Amanda or Dr. Crider and answer the character study questions in relation to the chosen character.

Incorporate the responses in a written personality profile of the character.

Read aloud and discuss the profiles. What were the differences in the students' interpretations?

EVALUATION:
Can the student use guidance questions to gain information about a character? Can the student analyze actions of the character and formulate an accurate personality profile?

Respond

A LION TO GUARD US

Character Study Questionnaire

1. Is your character someone who actually lived, could likely exist or was imagined for the story?

2. Who are the other characters? Are they actual people or are they fictitious?

3. What does your character's speech, actions, ideas and appearance tell you about him or her?

4. What reasons does your character have for the things he or she does?

5. How do the other characters feel about your character?

6. Does your character have an opportunity to learn anything in the story?

7. How will your character be remembered? What characteristics or personalities about your character will stick in the mind's of readers the most?

A LION TO GUARD US

SUMMARY OF RESPONSE:
Compose and complete comparative graphs reflecting evaluations based on story plot and character knowledge.

OBJECTIVE:
- The student will use details to create a list of reasons.
- The student will create a graph to reflect the variety of responses.

THINKING LEVEL:
- Analysis
- Synthesis

MATERIALS:
- Literature selection
- Chalkboard
- Chalk

PREPARATION:
- Complete reading through chapter seven of the literature selection.
- Divide the chalkboard into two sections. Label one **Go** and the other one **Stay**.

RESPONSE INSTRUCTIONS:
Amanda and her siblings are homeless, penniless and orphaned. To go to the New World they need money or an adult to take them. The difficult journey across the ocean is dangerous. What are their chances for survival?

Brainstorm two lists. One list will be reasons for Amanda and her siblings to go to the New World. The second list will be reasons for them to stay in London. The student recorder writes the responses in the correct sections on the chalkboard.

Create two graphs by polling the students in each category. Which reason do they **most** agree with? Discuss the results of the poll by reading the graphs.

EVALUATION:
Can the student use details from story content to create a list of reasons for Amanda to stay in London and for her to go to the New World? Is the student able to interpret a graph?

A LION TO GUARD US

SUMMARY OF RESPONSE:
Form cooperative groups to rewrite and illustrate the story outcome based on an alternative chapter ending.

OBJECTIVE:
- The student will propose plot changes.
- The student will rewrite plot outcomes based on these changes.

THINKING LEVEL:
- Application
- Synthesis

MATERIALS:
- Large sheet white construction paper
- Pencils
- Crayons

PREPARATION:
- Review chapter seven in the literature selection.
- Divide into cooperative groups of four.
- Distribute a sheet of construction paper to each group.

RESPONSE INSTRUCTIONS:

The plot direction at the end of chapter seven is reflected in the chapter title. Discuss the "piece of luck" that came the children's way. How did this "piece of luck" change their lives?

Instruct students to fold the construction paper into four equal sections. The first student writes an alternative ending to chapter seven. Perhaps the children met a different person or were led somewhere else. Pass the paper to the next student who writes a sentence or two that continues the story based on the newly proposed ending. Continue to pass the paper until all sections are filled and each student has contributed. Decide on a new title for the chapter. Illustrate each section.

Compare the proposed plot changes with actual story events.

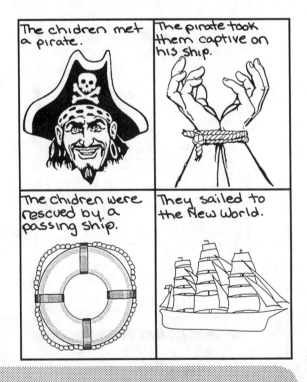

The children met a pirate.

The pirate took them captive on his ship.

The children were rescued by a passing ship.

They sailed to the New World.

EVALUATION:
Can the student propose an alternate ending and logical plot outcomes based on the alternative? Can students work cooperatively to compose an alternate plot?

A LION TO GUARD US

SUMMARY OF RESPONSE:
Complete a story map that reflects the sequence of events in the plot that relates specifically to problems faced by the main characters.

OBJECTIVE:
- The student will identify a problem based on story content.
- The student will use a story map in order to track the sequence of events that relate to the problem.

THINKING LEVEL:
- Knowledge
- Application

MATERIALS:
- Story map, following
- Pencils

PREPARATION:
- Reproduce and distribute a story map to each student.

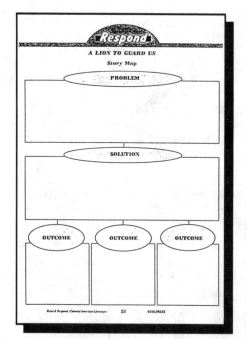

RESPONSE INSTRUCTIONS:
Throughout the book there are problems and challenges that Amanda must contend with in order to take care of her brother and sister. Have students identify some of the problems then choose one to track sequentially in the story map.

Upon completion, discuss what the student might have done if he or she were Amanda.

EVALUATION:
Can the student identify problems presented in the story? Can the problem, its solution and its outcomes be reflected sequentially in a story map?

A LION TO GUARD US

Story Map

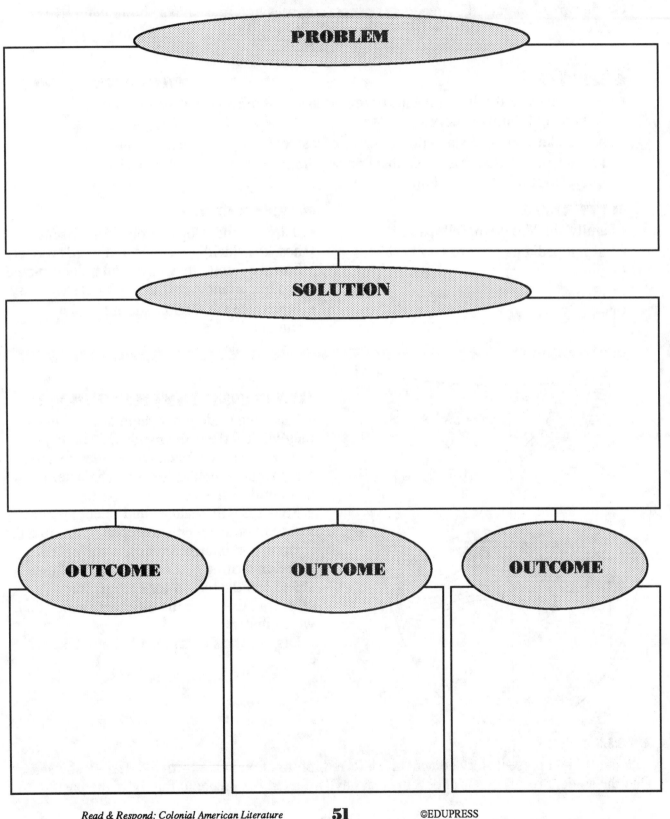

PROBLEM

SOLUTION

OUTCOME

OUTCOME

OUTCOME

Respond

A LION TO GUARD US

SUMMARY OF RESPONSE:
Use information gained by reading the literature selection to design a shield that reflects the Freebold's family history.

OBJECTIVE:
- The student will recall four events of importance that reflect the Freebold family history.
- The student will understand the elements of a shield.
- The student will design a shield that portrays important content as it relates to the family in the story.

THINKING LEVEL:
- Knowledge
- Comprehension
- Synthesis

MATERIALS:
- Family shield pattern, following
- Encyclopedia pictures of family shields
- Pencil
- Crayons
- Drawing paper

PREPARATION:
- Share the encyclopedia pictures. Discuss how the shield's pictures and words reflect how the family may have gotten its surname and important events in the family's history.
- Reproduce the shield pattern for each student.

RESPONSE INSTRUCTIONS:
Ask each student to design a shield that they think reflects the Freebold's family history. They will need to consider specific story facts as well as inferred character traits and family values.

Students will evaluate and select the four most important events to depict in the shield.

Upon completion, invite the students to share, in writing or aloud, the story of their shield and the reason for each picture selection. Compare the different shields that were created.

Display the shields on a bulletin board.

EVALUATION:
Can the student present story content and inferred information in the form of a family shield?
Can the student recall important events that have affected the Freebold family in the past?

A LION TO GUARD US

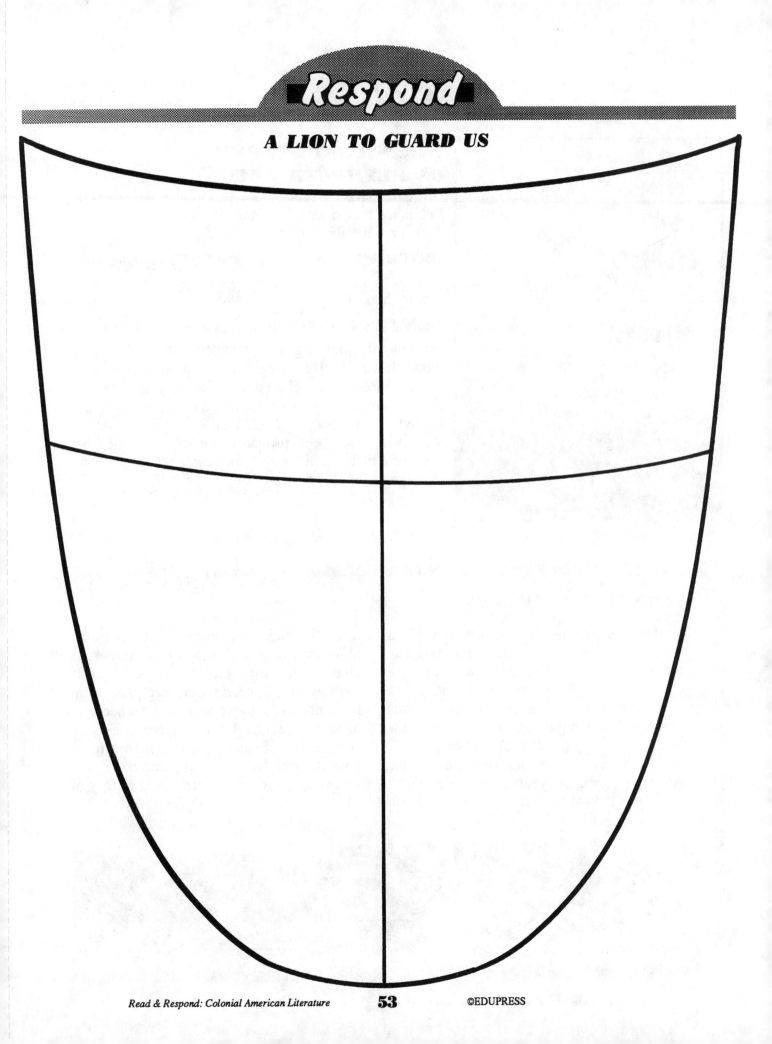

WHO'S THAT STEPPING ON PLYMOUTH ROCK?

by Jean Fritz
Published by Coward-McCann, 1975.
Canadian distribution by Bejo Sales.

DESCRIPTION:	READING LEVEL:
30 pages	Read aloud—Grades 3-4
Picture book	Independent—Grades 5-6

CONTENT NOTES:

Plymouth Rock, a granite boulder with the date 1620 carved on it, lies near the sea at Plymouth, Massachusetts. According to popular story, the Pilgrims on the Mayflower stepped ashore on this rock when they landed in America on December 21, 1620. While the story has never been proven to be true, the rock has become a national historic monument, a testament to the courage of the Pilgrim settlers.

CONTENT SUMMARY:

Here is the humanizing account of an important piece of American heritage. The book takes the reader through the adventurous life of Plymouth Rock.

The reader first meets this now-famous rock as it sits in the sea, home only to a few passing sea gulls. Then along comes 1620 and the rock's life is changed forever. One hundred twenty years after the "First Comers'" landing, city Elders decide to make the rock a landmark. Thus begins the many amazing and sometimes humorous changes the rock undergoes. A wharf is built around it, celebrations are planned in its honor and a move to a more respectable area proves to be more trouble than imagined. Finally, a monument is constructed to house it. Learn all the amusing anecdotes that follow the story of Plymouth Rock through over 350 years.

WHO'S THAT STEPPING ON PLYMOUTH ROCK?

SUMMARY OF RESPONSE:
Participate in a pre-reading activity that builds awareness of the network of associations connected with Plymouth Rock.

OBJECTIVE:
- The student will share ideas based on personal experience.
- The student will identify associations relating to the network of knowledge surrounding Plymouth Rock.

THINKING LEVEL:
- Knowledge
- Comprehension

MATERIALS:
- Chalkboard
- Chalk

PREPARATION:
- Select a student to be a recorder.

RESPONSE INSTRUCTIONS:
Approach this pre-reading strategy by asking the students what comes to mind when they hear the words, "Plymouth Rock." Ask the student recorder to write the shared ideas on the chalkboard.

The second stage of this lesson involves asking the students, "What made you think of that?" During this time, students develop new or different associations as they listen to the responses of others. As students learn more from the class interactions, they may modify earlier associations.

The third stage is one of reformulations. Students tell any new ideas about Plymouth Rock based on the class discussion. All of these discussions are recorded.

EVALUATION:
Can the student draw ideas from previous knowledge regarding Plymouth Rock in order to become aware of the network of knowledge surrounding Plymouth Rock?

WHO'S THAT STEPPING ON PLYMOUTH ROCK?

SUMMARY OF RESPONSE:
Work in cooperative pairs to complete a "cause and effect" study of community actions throughout Plymouth Rock's history.

OBJECTIVE:
- The student will understand the concept of "cause and effect".
- The student will apply the concept to actions taken by the community around Plymouth Rock.

THINKING LEVEL:
- Comprehension
- Application

MATERIALS:
- Cause and Effect Worksheet, following
- Pencil

PREPARATION:
- Divide into cooperative pairs.
- Reproduce the Cause and Effect Worksheet and distribute one to each pair of students.
- Prepare examples that illustrate the concept of "cause and effect".

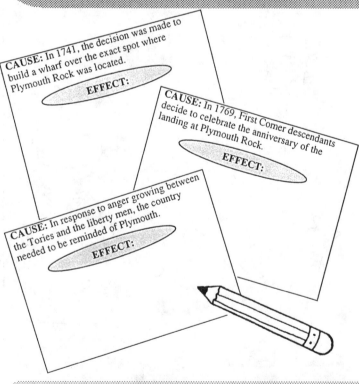

CAUSE: In 1741, the decision was made to build a wharf over the exact spot where Plymouth Rock was located.
EFFECT:

CAUSE: In 1769, First Comer descendants decide to celebrate the anniversary of the landing at Plymouth Rock.
EFFECT:

CAUSE: In response to anger growing between the Tories and the liberty men, the country needed to be reminded of Plymouth.
EFFECT:

RESPONSE INSTRUCTIONS:
Review the concept of "cause and effect". When the concept is understood, the students are ready to complete the worksheet.

Work in pairs to discuss and respond to the **Cause** statement on the worksheet. The literature selection may be referred to, if necessary.

When responses are finished, combine as a class to discuss the answers. At this point, other effects may be discussed. How would these possibilities affect America's history?

EVALUATION:
Can the student determine and write the effects of decisions and actions taken by the community around Plymouth Rock? Can the student work cooperatively with others?

WHO'S THAT STEPPING ON PLYMOUTH ROCK?

Cause and Effect Worksheet

CAUSE: In 1741, the decision was made to build a wharf over the exact spot where Plymouth Rock was located.

EFFECT:

CAUSE: In 1769, First Comer descendants decide to celebrate the anniversary of the landing at Plymouth Rock.

EFFECT:

CAUSE: In response to anger growing between the Tories and the liberty men, the country needed to be reminded of Plymouth.

EFFECT:

CAUSE: On December 22, the people of Plymouth decided to move the rock. They used the strongest men, tools and oxen.

EFFECT:

CAUSE: The people of Plymouth decide they couldn't leave such a famous rock lying loose under an elm tree.

EFFECT:

CAUSE: In 1920, it was the 300th anniversary of the Landing. The community decided to move the monument to a bigger and nicer place.

EFFECT:

Respond

WHO'S THAT STEPPING ON PLYMOUTH ROCK?

SUMMARY OF RESPONSE:
Make a time line to reflect Plymouth Rock's 350-year-history by placing illustrations in sequential order. Describe the events depicted in each illustration.

OBJECTIVE:
- The student will recall a sequence of events according to the literature selection.
- The student will place the illustrations in the correct sequence to form a time line of Plymouth Rock's history.

THINKING LEVEL:
- Knowledge
- Synthesis

MATERIALS:
- Time line illustrations, following
- Construction paper
- Scissors
- Glue or paste
- Crayons

PREPARATION:
- Reproduce and distribute the time line illustrations to each student.
- Cut a full sheet of construction paper in half lengthwise. Give one-half to each student.

RESPONSE INSTRUCTIONS:

Ask students to make a time line of Plymouth Rock's history beginning in 1620 and continuing for 350 years through to the end of the literature selection.

Fold the half-sheet of construction paper into eight equal-sized boxes. Number each box in the top left corner as shown below. Cut apart the illustrations on the solid lines. Arrange them in sequential order onto the half-sheet of construction paper. Color and glue the illustrations in place. Students may write a short description below each illustration. Incorporate dates into the description.

EVALUATION:
Is the student able to place illustrations in sequential order to create a time line of Plymouth Rock's history? Is the student able to write a corresponding description?

WHO'S THAT STEPPING ON PLYMOUTH ROCK?

SUMMARY OF RESPONSE:
Pretend you are Plymouth Rock and write an autobiography to publish for interested historians.

OBJECTIVE:
- The student will imagine that he/she is Plymouth Rock.
- The student will write a first-person narrative.
- The student will write from the perspective of an inanimate object.

THINKING LEVEL:
- Synthesis
- Synthesis
- Application

MATERIALS:
- Autobiography form, following
- Pen or pencil
- Construction paper
- Stapler
- Crayons

PREPARATION:
- Review the elements of an autobiography.
- Reproduce and distribute one autobiography form to each student. Have extra forms on hand for lengthier accounts.

RESPONSE INSTRUCTIONS:
Be sure the students understand the elements of an autobiography. Ask them to imagine they are Plymouth Rock. Briefly brainstorm some of the events that occurred in their lifetime. Focus on turning points, memorable events and important dates.

Use the form provided on which to write the autobiography. The events shared may be different for each student. More pages may be added if necessary.

When complete, design a construction paper cover and staple it to the written pages. Share the published autobiographies in an authors' corner.

EVALUATION:
Can the student imagine that they are Plymouth Rock? Can the student write in the first-person narrative from the perspective of Plymouth Rock?

WHO'S THAT STEPPING ON PLYMOUTH ROCK?

My Autobiography...

_____

_____

_____

_____

_____

_____

_____

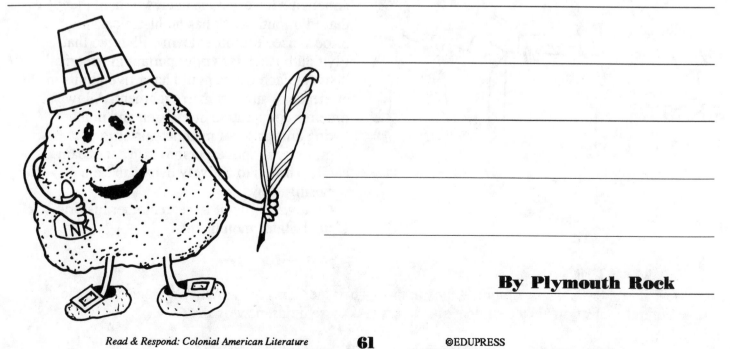

_____

_____

_____

By Plymouth Rock

Respond

WHO'S THAT STEPPING ON PLYMOUTH ROCK?

SUMMARY OF RESPONSE:

Conduct an organized debate in which two cooperative teams argue the importance of Plymouth Rock in American history.

OBJECTIVE:

- The student will apply the elements of debate.
- The student will defend a position regarding the importance of Plymouth Rock in our history.

THINKING LEVEL:

- Application
- Evaluation

MATERIALS:

- Index cards
- Pen
- Research materials

PREPARATION:

- Discuss the elements of a debate. Practice supporting an opinion with fact.
- Divide students into two teams.

RESPONSE INSTRUCTIONS:

Be sure students understand the elements of a debate. Explain they will debate the issue of the importance of Plymouth Rock in America's history. One team will hold the idea that Plymouth Rock has no historical importance. The other team will argue that Plymouth Rock is very important in America's history. Each team should have five points of evidence to support their argument. Allow time for cooperative discussion and note-taking among team members prior to beginning. A spokesperson from each team can be chosen to actively debate these opposing views.

Optional activity: Research other historic United States monuments.

EVALUATION:

Is the student able to support a position on an issue using information gained from the literature selection? Is the student able to express these opinions verbally?

WHO'S THAT STEPPING ON PLYMOUTH ROCK?

SUMMARY OF RESPONSE:
Conduct a question-and-answer activity in which the questions based on the literature selection are formulated by students.

OBJECTIVE:
- The student will develop questions based on story content.
- The student will answer questions generated by another student.

THINKING LEVEL:
- Application
- Comprehension

MATERIALS:
- Literature selection
- Paper
- Pencil

PREPARATION:
- Determine stopping points throughout the literature selection. Allow a few pages of reading between each question-and-answer session.
- Provide students with paper and pencil.

RESPONSE INSTRUCTIONS:

Read the text aloud to the class. At the predetermined stopping points, students write two or three questions based on the reading.

Randomly select several students to read aloud a question they have composed. They may call on a classmate to answer it. If the students would like an expanded answer, he or she may call on another student. Answers should be supported with details from the text.

This strategy may continue through the entire reading or be implemented for portions of the literature selection.

EVALUATION:
Can the student compose questions that are appropriate to story content? Is the student able to answer questions using content information to support the response?

Exciting Learning for Grades 3-6 from **Edupress**

127 Report Form Roundup $8.95

Build report writing skills with ready-to-use forms—people, places, books & more.

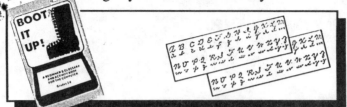

201 Boot It Up $1.25

A beginner's glossary & activity book for the computer.

211 Cursive Companion $1.98

4x8 non-stick, desktop aids for handwriting mastery; 32 per pack.

134 Oodles of Writing $7.95

Hundreds of quick-pick topics, starters & formats develop the writing process.

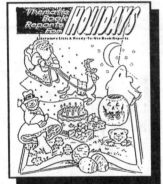

155 Book Reports/Holiday $6.95

Thematic bibliographies and ready-to-use book report forms for holidays.

156 Book Reports/Math $6.95

Bibliographies and ready-to-use book report forms relating to math themes.

157 Book Reports/Science $6.95

Thematic bibliographies and ready-to-use book report forms relating to science.

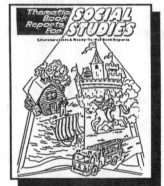

158 Book Reports/Soc Stu $6.95

Bibliographies and ready-to-use book report forms for social studies themes.

128 Easy Book Projects $6.95

Lots of motivating activities for exploring, sharing & reporting on books.

Quick Learning Kits $8.95 each

141 Math & Science **142 Language & Social Studies** **143 Art & Literature**

Directions, tips & tools for making interactive, multicurricular learning kits from recyclables. 40 kits in each book.

108 Triple Treat $4.95

Write, create, decorate! 20 Go-together story, art and bulletin board ideas.

117 Wonders of Nature $4.95

Three theme units based on a reading selection: *coral reef, snow, chameleons.*

109 Vocabulary Challenge $6.95

Weekly vocabulary enrichment program—tests, review, reinforcement.

161 Ancient Egypt Activities $5.95

Art, crafts, cooking & historical aids provide an active glimpse of the past.